The
World
of
Friendship

The World of Friendship

EDITED BY
JAYNE BOWMAN

A READER'S DIGEST/C.R. GIBSON BOOK

Published by The C.R. Gibson Company, Norwalk, Connecticut 06856

A Reader's Digest/C.R.Gibson book published by arrangement with The Reader's Digest Association, Inc., Pleasantville, N.Y., 10570.

Printed in the United States of America.

ISBN: 0-8378-1801-X

Contents

Introduction

Friendships come in a wonderful variety. Some, born of our early years, endure for a lifetime — deepening and growing richer with each passing year. Others bloom brightly until, separated by a move or change of job, we lose touch with one another. But the memories of such friendships remain fresh — as cherished as photographs in treasured albums. At other times, when we are in the midst of trouble or sorrow, strangers may reach out to us in compassion. This, too, is friendship. We accept such acts of friendship with gratefulness and more than a little awe.

Today, more than ever, we have a wonderful opportunity to forge friendships. In a world grown small through the advent of high-speed aircraft, we are able to meet many people from different cities, different lands, different cultures. Such friendships add a new dimension to our lives, something of value that would not have been there had we never met. When friends share with us their thoughts, their experiences, their way of looking at the world, our own vision is extended and enhanced.

The world of friendship — it is a world of caring and sharing — a world of adventures and memories. It is a very special gift and a very special joy.

I

*A
Friend
Is
Someone
Special*

"Yonder's My Best Friend"

An idyl of a boyhood friendship whose imprint has remained undiminished by the years.

The first time I saw him was in early September, when the days have finished the slow, pleasant climb up the steep hill of summer and suddenly whiz downward at a terrifying speed toward the opening of school.

He leaned casually against a giant cottonwood, dressed in a muddy T-shirt and faded blue jeans, half cloth, half holes. A slingshot, obviously carved by a skilled young warrior, dangled from the one remaining hip pocket, and with his bare toes he picked up stones and sent them spinning, a talent that can be developed only after many shoeless months. He wasn't tall and he wasn't short, but his shoulders were broad and his deeply tanned legs and arms seemed overly muscular for an eight-year-old.

As the new boy in town, I studied him with the eyes of self-preservation, attempting to discover what form my indoctrination in this central Texas community would take — wrestling, fistfighting, foot racing or talking. While I squirmed with apprehension, he calmly watched a bird flutter into the cottonwood. He studied it intently, then turned to me with a grin that seemed to split his face in half. "Jaybird," he said. "Mighty pretty thing, but watch that old squawker when it's got a baby. Mean as heck."

With that he strolled over and squatted down a few yards in front of me. "I live over yonder," he said. "My name's Claudius. C-l-a-u-d-i-u-s. 'Fore you ask, my mother's a big 'un for reading books. That's where she got it — outta some book. And don't go asking me what book 'cause I don't know."

For the next few minutes he was immobile, his eyes riveted on an ant that stumbled along with a hefty load through the yet unmowed grass. Then, with a motion as graceful as the flight of a kite in a summer breeze, he was upright, a hand shading his face and his eyes darting toward the sun.

"The sun says it's two o'clock — way past dinnertime," he said. I glanced at my birthday wrist watch; the hands pointed to ten minutes after two. "Come on, we got some cold quail in the icebox."

To him, it was that simple. We were to be friends.

For the next six years, Claudius was to fill that one great need of childhood: to be able to point to someone and say, "Yonder's my best friend." To him, friendship was a pledge of loyalty and unselfishness, given without question or motive. He gladly shared his knowledge of the outdoors without the usual childhood bragging or intimidation. He taught me to fish for crawdads with a hunk of bacon and a bent pin, to name every wild flower on the hillsides, to swing from a vine over Little River and drop into the exact spot where the current would carry you downstream for a quarter of a mile and deposit you on the slippery, muddy bank.

On the day I was to try the vine-swinging act for the first time, my stomach churned with fear, and I couldn't move. Several playmates began to taunt: "Look there, he's scared to even try it." "You ain't getting yellow, are you?"

Claudius came up the muddy bank and stood next to me. He whispered, "It's just the getting around to doing that scares you, not the doing." He yelled down to those taunting me from the water, "Watch out below! We're going to do something that's never been done before. We're going to swing out on this one little vine together and then drop off. We dare any of you all to do it."

We swung with a belly-sinking arc over the water as the vine strained under our weight. We turned loose and drifted downward as if in one of those falling nightmares until we knifed through the water, bobbed to the surface, and spun downstream to the landing place. The others spread the word the next day of our daring.

With Claudius I tasted my first turtle-egg soup, first rabbit stew, first blackbird pie, and first bean-hole beans — a taste memory that still awakens me at night with a hunger that could only be sated with this culinary miracle of pinto beans, tomatoes, onions and bacon, cooked in a can buried deep in the ground over smoldering coals. We became experts at climbing the six-foot-high picket fence surrounding the big house in the next block and removing the green plums and peaches, which, with one firm bite, would turn your lip over your nose, and often as not your stomach over your liver.

One lazy, nothing-to-do afternoon, conversation among a group of our classmates developed into a debate on the fighting ability of those attending the local grade school. Never especially strong, I did have tenacity, developed for no other reason than that my father was the high-school football coach in a football-crazy town. This alone made it necessary for me to defend my honor, and his, on many occasions, especially during losing seasons. I had won many victories, and a reputation, through bullheadedness alone, and I had a scar on my chin and another on my nose to prove my worth. Claudius had not been compelled to prove *his* worth since the day he was pushed into a fight with the largest boy in the class and had crushed the bully into the playground dust.

As the clamor for a showdown increased, I yielded to social pressure and announced that we'd settle it with a wrestling match, as best friends shouldn't fistfight. Claudius, who had been silent throughout the argument, rose slowly, peeled off his shirt, and said, "Let's go, but I still don't know why."

Three hours later, the contest was called a draw. Both of us were scratched, skinned, bloody, sweaty and grass-stained. Claudius turned toward home, while I listened to the praises of the hangers-on. Just once Claudius looked at me. With saddened eyes, he said softly, "Friends don't have to prove nothing to nobody, much less to each other."

As the passing years added a few grams of wisdom here and there, I realized that had he expended all his strength, the three-hour match would have ended in 15 minutes.

Claudius and I parted in our early teens when my family moved. We attempted to keep the friendship alive with summer visits, exchanges of Christmas gifts — mine generally purchased, his always a handmade wonder — and an occasional letter from me. "What can you tell a friend," he'd say, explaining why he never wrote, "by putting words down on paper and not even knowing if he understands what you mean?"

Then, one Thanksgiving Day, I sat in the locker room awaiting the opening kickoff of a high-school championship football game. My stomach was churning with pre-game nervousness when Claudius strolled into the steaming room. He had given up turkey and dressing with his family and hitchhiked 125 miles to see the game.

After the coach had given the final instructions and we waited in apprehension to take the field, Claudius leaned forward and, with the grin that seemed to split his face in half, said, "Watch them jaybirds when they get the ball. Mean as heck!"

It was enough to send me out free of nervousness and untroubled by the screams of the spectators or the blare of the bands.

When the contest was over, I knelt near the center of the field, too exhausted, too numb, to move. One eye was red-rimmed with tears, the other already swollen shut and turning blue-black. We had lost, 19-18.

I was oblivious to everything until Claudius slapped my helmet with his palm and said, "It won't be long until people can't even remember who won and who lost. But you keep your score in your own head. You did better than your best today, and that's all you need to remember. The way I figure it, you won."

We walked off the field together, one sweat-stained and beaten, the other striding as if with the champions.

It has been more than three decades since I've seen Claudius or the old Texas cottonwood. It's been that long since I've really listened to the chatter of a mockingbird, or the clatter of a tin can kicked by a bare foot.

But it was only yesterday that I advised a youngster, "Friends don't have to prove nothing to nobody, much less to each other." And it was only today I reminded myself, once again, that "it's just the getting around to doing that scares you, not the doing."

What's more, I still keep my own score in my own head, and that way, a lot of times, I figure I'm a winner.

ROB WOOD

Oh, the comfort, the inexpressible comfort,
of feeling safe with a person; having neither
to weigh thoughts nor measure words, but to
pour them all out just as they are, chaff and
grain together, knowing that a faithful hand
will take and sift them, keep what is worth
keeping, and then, with the breath of
kindness, blow the rest away.

DINAH MARIA MULOCK CRAIK

The Stranger Who Taught Magic

"You're a boy willing to teach; I'm a teacher willing to learn." For one shining summer, a boy who loved a world of salt water and sea creatures and a teacher who loved a world of words and ideas shared a unique friendship.

That July morning was like any other, calm and opalescent before the heat of the fierce Georgia sun. I was 13: sunburned, shaggy-haired, a little aloof, and solitary. In winter I had to put on shoes and go to school like everyone else. But summers I lived by the sea, and my mind was empty and wild and free.

On this particular morning, I had tied my rowboat to the pilings of an old dock upriver from our village. There, sometimes, the striped sheepshead lurked in the still, green water. I was crouched, motionless as a stone, when a voice spoke suddenly above my head: "Canst thou draw out leviathan with a hook, or his tongue with a cord which thou lettest down?"

I looked up, startled, into a lean, pale face and a pair of the most remarkable eyes I had ever seen. It wasn't a question of color. It was a combination of things: warmth, humor, interest, alertness. Intensity — that's the word, I guess — and, underlying it all, a curious kind of mocking sadness. I believe I thought him old.

He saw how taken aback I was. "Sorry," he said. "It's a bit early in the morning for the Book of Job, isn't it?" He nodded at the two or three fish in the boat. "Think you could teach me how to catch those?"

Ordinarily, I was wary of strangers, but anyone interested in fishing was hardly a stranger. I nodded, and he climbed down into the boat. "Perhaps we should introduce ourselves," he said. "But then again, perhaps not. You're a boy willing to teach; I'm a teacher willing to learn. That's introduction enough. I'll call you 'Boy,' and you call me 'Sir.' "

Such talk sounded strange in my world of sun and salt water. But there was something so magnetic about the man, and so disarming about his smile, that I didn't care.

I handed him a hand line and showed him how to bait his hooks with fiddler crabs. He told me he had rented one of the weathered bungalows behind the dock. "I needed to hide for a while," he said. "Not from the police, or anything like that. Just from friends and relatives. So don't tell anyone you've found me, will you?"

I asked what he taught.

"In the school catalogue they call it English," he said. "But I like to think of it as a course in magic — in the mystery and magic of words. Are you fond of words?"

I said that I had never thought much about them. I also pointed out that the tide was ebbing, that the current was too strong for more fishing, and that in any case it was time for breakfast.

"Of course," he said, pulling in his line. "I'm a little

forgetful about such things these days." He eased himself back onto the dock with a little grimace, as if the effort cost him something. "Will you be back on the river later?"

I said that I would probably go casting for shrimp at low tide.

"Stop by," he said. "We'll talk about words for a while, and then perhaps you can show me how to catch shrimp."

So began a most unlikely friendship, because I did go back. To this day, I'm not sure why. Perhaps it was because, for the first time, I had met an adult on terms that were in balance. In the realm of words and ideas, he might be the teacher. But in my own small universe of winds and tides and sea creatures, the wisdom belonged to me.

Almost every day after that, we'd go wherever the sea gods or my whim decreed. Sometimes up the silver creeks, where the terrapin skittered down the banks and the great blue herons stood like statues. Sometimes along the ocean dunes, fringed with graceful sea oats, where by night the great sea turtles crawled and by day the wild goats browsed. I showed him where the mullet swirled and where the flounder lay in cunning camouflage. I learned that he was incapable of much exertion; even pulling up the anchor seemed to exhaust him. But he never complained. And, all the time, talk flowed from him like a river.

Much of it I have forgotten now, but some comes back as clear and distinct as if it all happened yesterday. "Words," he'd say. "Just little black marks on paper. Just sounds in the empty air. But think of the power they have! They can make you laugh or cry, love or hate, fight or run away. They can heal or hurt. They even come to look and sound like what they mean. Angry *looks* angry on the page. Ugly *sounds* ugly when you say it.

Or "Rhythm," he would say. "Life is full of it; words should have it, too. But you have to train your ear. Listen to the waves on a quiet night; you'll pick up the cadence. Look at the patterns the wind makes in dry sand and you'll see how syllables in a sentence should fall. Do you know what I mean?"

My conscious self didn't know; but perhaps something deep inside me did. In any case, I listened.

I listened, too, when he read from the books he sometimes brought. Often he would stop and repeat a phrase or a line that pleased him. One day, in Malory's *Le Morte d'Arthur*, he found one: "And the great horse grimly neighed." "Close your eyes," he said to me, "and say that slowly, out loud." I did. "How did it make you feel?" "It gives me the shivers," I said truthfully. He was delighted.

But the magic that he taught was not confined to words; he had a way of generating in me an excitement about things I had always taken for granted. He might point to a bank of clouds. "What do you see there? Colors? That's not enough. Look for towers and drawbridges. Look for dragons and griffins and strange and wonderful beasts."

Or he might pick up an angry, claw-brandishing blue crab, holding it cautiously by the back flippers as I had taught him. "Pretend you're this crab," he'd say.

19

"What do you see through those stalk-like eyes? What do you feel with those complicated legs? What goes on in your tiny brain? Try it for just five seconds. Stop being a boy. Be a crab!" And I would stare in amazement at the furious creature, feeling my comfortable identity lurch and sway under the impact of the idea.

So the days went by. Our excursions became less frequent, because he tired so easily. He brought two chairs down to the dock and some books, but he didn't read much. He seemed content to watch me as I fished, or the circling gulls, or the slow river coiling past.

A sudden shadow fell across my life when my parents told me I was going to camp for two weeks. On the dock that afternoon I asked my friend if he would be there when I got back. "I hope so," he said gently.

But he wasn't. I remember standing on the sun-warmed planking of the old dock, staring at the shuttered bungalow and feeling a hollow sense of finality and loss. I ran to Jackson's grocery store — where everyone knew everything — and asked where the schoolteacher had gone.

"He was sick, real sick," Mrs. Jackson replied. "Doc phoned his relatives up north to come get him. He left something for you — he figured you'd be asking after him."

She handed me a book. It was a slender volume of verse, *Flame and Shadow*, by someone I had never heard of: Sara Teasdale. The corner of one page was turned down, and there was a penciled star by one of the poems. I still have the book, with that poem, "On the Dunes."*

> *If there is any life when death is over,*
>   *These tawny beaches will know much of me,*
> *I shall come back, as constant and as changeful*
>   *As the unchanging, many-colored sea.*
> *If life was small, if it has made me scornful,*
>   *Forgive me; I shall straighten like a flame*
> *In the great calm of death, and if you want me*
>   *Stand on the sea-ward dunes and call my name.*

Well, I have never stood on the dunes and called his name. For one thing, I never knew it; for another, I'd be too self-conscious. And there are long stretches when I forget all about him. But sometimes — when the music or the magic in a phrase makes my skin tingle, or when I pick up an angry blue crab, or when I see a dragon in the flaming sky — sometimes I remember.

ARTHUR GORDON

*Reprinted with permission of the Macmillan Co.

When I see an honored friend again after years of separation, it is like resuming the words of an old conversation which had been halted momentarily by time. Surely as one gets older, friendship becomes more precious to us, for it affirms the contours of our existence. It is a reservoir of shared experience, of having lived through many things in our brief and mutual moment on earth.

WILLIE MORRIS

Information Please

He was a young boy, and she was a telephone operator. Theirs was a very special friendship.

When I was quite young my family had one of the first telephones in our neighborhood. I remember well the polished oak case fastened to the wall on the lower stair landing. I was too little to reach the telephone but used to listen with fascination when my mother talked to it.

Then I discovered that somewhere inside that wonderful device lived an amazing person — her name was "Information Please" and there was nothing she did not know. My mother could ask her for anybody's number; when our clock ran down, Information Please immediately supplied the correct time.

My first personal experience with this genie-in-the-receiver came one day while my mother was visiting a neighbor. Amusing myself at the tool-bench in the basement, I whacked my finger with a hammer. The pain was terrible, but there didn't seem to be much use crying because there was no one home to offer sympathy. I walked around the house sucking my throbbing finger, finally arriving at the stairway. The telephone! Quickly I ran for the footstool in the parlor and dragged it to the landing. Climbing up, I unhooked the receiver and held it to my ear. "Information Please," I said into the mouthpiece just above my head.

A small, clear voice spoke into my ear. "Information."

"I hurt my *finger*rrr —" I wailed into the phone. The tears came readily enough, now that I had an audience.

"Isn't your mother home?" came the question.

"Nobody's home but me," I blubbered.

"Are you bleeding?"

"No," I replied. "I hit it with the hammer and it hurts."

"Can you open your icebox?" she asked. I said I could. "Then chip off a little piece of ice and hold it on your finger. That will stop the hurt. Be careful when you use the ice pick," she admonished. "And don't cry. You'll be all right."

After that, I called Information Please for everything. I asked her for help with my geography and she told me where Philadelphia was, and the Orinoco — the romantic river I was going to explore when I grew up. She helped me with my arithmetic, and she told me that my pet chipmunk — I had caught him in the park just the day before — would eat fruit and nuts.

And there was the time that Petey, our pet canary, died. I called Information Please and told her the sad story. She listened, then said the usual things grown-ups say to soothe a child. But I was unconsoled: why was it that birds should sing so beautifully and bring joy to whole families, only to end as a heap of feathers, feet up, on the bottom of a cage?

She must have sensed my deep concern, for she said quietly, "Paul, always remember that there are other worlds to sing in."

Somehow I felt better.

Another day I was at the telephone. "Information," said the now familiar voice.

"How do you spell fix?" I asked.

"Fix something? F-i-x."

At that instant my sister, who took unholy joy in scaring me, jumped off the stairs at me with a banshee shriek — "*Yaaaaaaaaaa!*" I fell off the stool, pulling the receiver out of the box by its roots. We were both terrified — Information Please was no longer there, and I was not at all sure that I hadn't hurt her when I pulled the receiver out.

24

Minutes later there was a man on the porch. "I'm a telephone repairman," he said. "I was working down the street and the operator said there might be some trouble at this number." He reached for the receiver in my hand. "What happened?"

I told him.

"Well, we can fix that in a minute or two." He opened the telephone box and fiddled for a while with the end of the receiver cord, tightening things with a small screwdriver. He jiggled the hook up and down a few times, then spoke into the phone. "Hi, this is Pete. Everything's under control. The kid's sister scared him and he pulled the cord out of the box."

All this took place in a small town in the Pacific Northwest. Then, when I was nine years old, we moved across the country to Boston — and I missed my mentor acutely. Information Please belonged in that old wooden box back home, and I somehow never thought of trying the new phone that sat on a small table in the hall.

Yet, as I grew into my teens, the memories of those childhood conversations never really left me; often in moments of doubt and perplexity I would recall the serene sense of security I had when I knew that I could call Information Please and get the right answer. I appreciated now how very patient, understanding and kind she was to have wasted her time on a little boy.

A few years later, on my way west to college, my plane put down at Seattle. I had about half an hour between plane connections, and I spent 15 minutes or so on the phone with my sister, who lived there now, happily mellowed by marriage and motherhood. Then, really without thinking what I was doing, I dialed my hometown operator and said, "Information Please."

Miraculously, I heard again the small, clear voice I knew so well: "Information."

I hadn't planned this, but I heard myself saying, "Could you tell me, please, how to spell the word 'fix'?"

There was a long pause. Then came the softly spoken answer. "I guess," said Information Please, "that your finger must have healed by now."

I laughed. "So it's really still you," I said. "I wonder if you have any idea how much you meant to me during all that time . . ."

"I wonder," she replied, "if you know how much you meant to *me*? I never had any children, and I used to look forward to your calls. Silly, wasn't it?"

It didn't seem silly, but I didn't say so. Instead, I told her how often I had thought of her over the years, and I asked if I could call her again when I came back to visit my sister after the first semester was over.

"Please do. Just ask for Sally."

"Good-by, Sally." It sounded strange for Information Please to have a name. "If I run into any chipmunks, I'll tell them to eat fruit and nuts."

"Do that," she said. "And I expect one of these days you'll be off for the Orinoco. Well, good-by."

Just three months later I was back again at the Seattle airport. A different voice answered, "Information," and I asked for Sally.

"Are you a friend?"

"Yes," I said. "An old friend."

"Then I'm sorry to have to tell you. Sally had only been working part-time in the last few years because she was ill. She died five weeks ago." But before I could hang up, she said, "Wait a minute. Did you say your name was Villiard?"

"Yes."

"Well, Sally left a message for you. She wrote it down."

"What was it?" I asked, almost knowing in advance what it would be.

"Here it is, I'll read it — 'Tell him I still say there are other worlds to sing in. He'll know what I mean.' "

I thanked her and hung up. I *did* know what Sally meant.

PAUL VILLIARD

Two little girls, one Jewish and the other Christian, were the very best of friends. After Easter the little Christian girl was asked by her grandfather what her best friend got for Easter. "Oh," she replied, "she didn't get anything for Easter. You see, I'm Easter and she's Passover. I'm Christmas and she's Hanukkah." Then with a big smile she added, "But we're both Halloween."

Contributed by D.R.R.

Friendship

With the falling of the leaves, the masks of green are stripped off the hillsides, revealing the diversity and uniqueness of each ridge and valley, rock and stream, old shed or oil well hitherto unseen. It is in the winter, when the hills bare their innermost selves, that we get to know them. Then, in the spring, when the masks return, we can look at the hills as old friends few others understand.

So it is with people. Most of the time we wear our masks. But during the difficult times, during the winters of our lives, we shed our facades and reveal all the intricacies of the unique beings we are. It is in these moments that friendships are formed, and we experience one another as few others ever will.

JOHN W. WALKER

II

Keep in Touch

Mail Call!

Rule One, for those who like to get letters, is: Who writes, receives.

"I miss letters!" sighed one of us at lunch. "Nobody writes them anymore. If it weren't for the weekend phone rates, we'd all be out of touch."

"But *Joan* writes letters," our host said.

The others turned to me. "You do? Tell us!"

I couldn't read. I knew just five letters of the alphabet: J, O, A, N and X. That was all I needed to print a mash note to Santa Claus.

"XXXXOOOO," I confided, breathing heavily on the paper. I filled the whole page with these sentiments, and signed with four colors of crayon. My mother addressed the envelope, I stamped it, and we walked the first letter of my life to the mailbox.

I knew nothing of geography, the limits of reality or the workings of the post office. But I comprehended that a letter could be loosed into the unknown and find its mark. That week I could hardly breathe for thinking of my letter in Santa's hand.

He wrote back. "A letter for you, Joanie," my mother called.

I opened it, trembling, and stared at the mysterious and beautiful shapes of words. Mother bent over me, and I followed her finger as she read the letter aloud to its extraordinary conclusion: "Merry Christmas and

XXXXOOOO! — Santa Claus." We looked at each other and popped our eyes.

"Read it again!" I said, and shivered.

That's how I learned the cardinal principle of correspondence: Who writes, receives. And to get a letter is one of life's incomparable joys.

I've been writing letters ever since, earning as I go the tremor of anticipation whenever I hear the creak of the mail truck as it turns our corner. What am I hoping to find? A new turn in a 20-year-old conversation, perhaps. A scene described. A question to set me pondering. A startle of surprise. Reassurance that the world still evenly turns and all is well.

Any letter could be one to make my day — or change my life. When I was 17, I opened an inviting letter that decided me on my choice of colleges. It followed that I met the man I married; lived where I did; had the children who are mine; and for years thought, felt, experienced and behaved according to a destiny that turned up in the morning mail.

Letters have sent me across America, into foreign wilderness, out to sea. Some of my richest friendships have been made and kept by letters alone — the faces never seen, the voices never heard. Letters eased me into my profession as a writer.

But if none of this had happened, I'd be writing letters anyway, and waiting for the mail. I love letters. I love *love* letters — all sorts of letters.

I love talk too. But talk I forget. Letters are tangible — to read and reread, to show around and share, or to tuck in a pocket and think about.

Letters have room in them for long pauses, reflection and rumination. They fatten on wit, philosophy, the recollected past and wished-for future. They are the expression of our human lonesomeness and sociability; the commitments we make—signed and sealed; the honor we pay to ceremony and significance.

I always smile at finding more to read in a letter than the words may say. There's no mistaking a proud man's grandiose capitals; the circles, arrows and asterisks of a cheerfully rococo mind; the lucid literacy of one who can type as fast as he thinks. A letter *is* who made it, even in appearance.

We should all write now and then, even when there's nothing much to say. It's enough to write about Sunday supper, violin lessons, the length of icicles, and the cat acting foolish.

I concede, it's not easy to find the time. My friends and I write wherever we happen to be when a lull falls ("The car's up on the lube rack and I'm...."). The letters go out with no obligations attached. No one keeps score or hints "You owe me!" There's pleasure in the writing itself, and that's it. Those who receive are touched, happily surprised, and will write back when they can, in their own good time.

It's marvelous how many letters are written in the serendipity of finding a half-hour so agreeable that it deserves to be shared. Right now, for instance. I'm nearly done with this and have nothing else pressing to do. And you?

JOAN MILLS

There are many people who practically never write to old friends, because they have a feeling that if they write at all they must write at length. But that is a great mistake; and by this indolent reticence many good ties are broken. The point is the letter, not the length or the literary quality of the letter. And it is pitiful to think that a few words scribbled on a scrap of paper three or four times in a year might save a good friendship perishing listlessly from lack of nutriment.

ARTHUR C. BENSON

A Letter to Walter

When this wonderful letter came from Walter, my old college pal, I had to restrain myself from going straight to the typewriter to let him know how much it meant to me. We hadn't seen each other since graduation, and hearing from him now brought back the carefree days of my youth. I knew at once that it would be foolish to rush into a reply — my letter would have to be every bit as special as his.

What a delightful letter he had sent me — high-spirited and full of fun like Walter himself! He recalled laughing girls we'd known and the time we had arrived for a house party in an ancient hearse that belonged to good old Chuck Weymouth. He mentioned the spring riot when Don Hartmann tried to borrow the fire truck.

My wife, of course, could not fully share my delight in these reminiscences of early bachelorhood; but, having my interests at heart, she reminded me several evenings later that I had not yet answered the letter. "You don't have to worry about my forgetting *that*," I assured her.

I aimed at Sunday afternoon — which came and went. "I was going to write Walter today," I remarked casually at dinner, "but I don't like to undertake it when I'm tired. You know, when you've been looking forward to something you don't want to spoil it by making drudgery out of it."

"Pass the salt," said my wife.

All that week I was buoyed up by the thought of the letter I was going to write. I could see Walter reading it with eyes alight, here and there laughing aloud. I myself wagged my head and chuckled just thinking about it. I didn't know exactly what I was going to say; but I knew how it was going to *sound*. It would be a classic of its kind.

Saturday came, and when my wife brought in the mail and said, "Incidentally, are you —" I replied quickly, "Right after dinner — that's when I'm going to get to it."

Unfortunately, that evening some friends came by — and stayed until bedtime.

It seemed that during the next week every little thing reminded me of the unanswered letter — any mention of college or old friends, or the mere word "letter." A chilling realization came upon me: the longer I put it off, the lengthier and more entertaining my letter was going to have to be to make up for the delay. It began to loom ahead of me like some kind of unscalable peak.

On Friday I came home with a bulging briefcase. I patted its flank jovially and observed that I had a lot of reading to do for the office.

"No letter to Walter this weekend?" was my wife's greeting.

"Certainly I'll write Walter if I find the time," I snapped. "But business comes first."

As the next week progressed, my unease and tension became more pronounced. The weekend brought no relief, for there seemed to be more demands on my time than ever. I had to paint all the flashing on the roof, which left time only to mow the lawn, read the

Sunday papers and get a bit of rest before going out to dinner.

By this time I felt thoroughly miserable. In replying to a letter like Walter's, one's frame of mind is everything, and I found myself incapable of summoning up the spontaneous, carefree, effervescent spirit the occasion demanded. "Hey, Walter, you old so-and-so, will you ever forget the time..." I'd try thinking of something like that only to recoil in despair. I became conscious of a great unseen Presence calling me to stern account, and I cowered under its unspoken and terrible rebuke. "Yes, I know, I *know*," I would plead, trying to shut my ears to it. "Look, I'm *going* to write that letter. But not *now*."

At last I turned resentful. Who was Walter Brenner to be putting me through all this? What right did he have to complicate my life with his breezy, inconsequential letter? It was easy to tell that Walter Brenner didn't have my problems — never did, in fact. He probably still lived in a big white house on a tree-shaded street, the same one he was born in. No mortgage, no trains to catch. No wonder he thought that I had unlimited leisure to give to a chatty, long-winded correspondence! The jam he had put me in had already taken up weeks. Yes, *weeks* had been spoiled by his thoughtlessness. Walter Brenner had always been a troublemaker.

Then one evening I came home to find a bottle of champagne in a bowl of ice beside a vase of roses on the coffee table. It took me a moment to remember, with a sinking feeling, that it was our wedding anniversary.

"Don't worry," declared the lady of the house. "It's just that you have such a lot on your mind. And think of the presents you're giving me — the champagne, the roses, dinner at Chez François."

A remarkable wife. But even as I toasted her she could see I was not rising to the occasion. "What's wrong?" she asked gently.

"Everything!" I exclaimed in despair. "My not remembering the date. The two books I've got that are overdue at the library. Four days at five cents each day! That's the way I am!" I cried. "What's money to me? I throw it away. I could give lessons to a drunken—"

"Hush," she said. "*I* have an anniversary present for *you*."

She was gone only a moment. When she returned she handed me a sheet of paper. It was a letter to Walter! A simple, friendly letter, beautifully typed, telling him how glad I'd been to hear from him and what I was doing at present. All it needed was my signature.

The Rock of Gibraltar was suddenly lifted from my back: embracing my wonderful wife in love and gratitude, I knew the pleasure, for the first time in long weeks, of being at peace with the world. After all, as I observed to her, there is nothing like the comfort and happiness to be found in keeping up with old friends.

"You didn't notice the 'Over' at the bottom of the page," she said.

On the other side was a postscript. It read: "I'll write again later at greater length."

I like to think that I was equal to the occasion: I

took my pen and hastily added "as soon as I've heard from you."

Then I leaned back and grinned. A grand friend, Walter—but let *him* suffer for a while.

CHARLTON OGBURN, JR.

In a small town I know, the postman makes one mistake time and again: when he has mail for a family that has just moved in, he always delivers it to another house in the same block. On discovering the "error," the neighbors take the mail to the new family — and real friendships often follow.

CLIFTON SIMER

The Thanksgiving Letters

We were a group of friends in the midst of an after-dinner conversation. Because Thanksgiving was just around the corner, we were talking about what we had to be thankful for.

One of us said: "Well I, for one, am grateful to Mrs. Wendt, an old schoolteacher who 30 years ago went out of her way to introduce me to Tennyson." She had, it appeared, awakened his literary interests and developed his gifts for expression.

"Does this Mrs. Wendt know that she made such a contribution to your life?" someone asked.

"I'm afraid not. I've never taken the trouble to tell her."

"Then why don't you write her? It would certainly make her happy, if she is alive, and it might make you happier, too. Far too few of us have developed the habit of gratitude."

All this was very poignant to me, because Mrs. Wendt was my teacher, and I was the fellow who hadn't written. My friend's challenge made me see that I had accepted something precious and hadn't bothered to say thanks.

That evening I wrote Mrs. Wendt what I called a Thanksgiving letter.

My letter was forwarded from town to town. Finally it reached her, and this is the note I had in return. It began:

"My dear Willie—"

That in itself was quite enough to warm my heart. Here was a man of 50, fat and bald, addressed as "Willie." I read on:

> I can't tell you how much your note meant to me. I am in my eighties, living alone in a small room, cooking my own meals, lonely and like the last leaf of fall lingering behind.
>
> You will be interested to know that I taught school for 50 years and yours is the first note of appreciation I ever received. It came on a blue, cold morning and it cheered me as nothing has in many years.

I confess I wept over that note.

My first Thanksgiving letter had proved so satisfying that I made a list of people who had contributed something deep and lasting to my life, and planned to write at least one every day in November. I sent out 50 letters. All but two brought answers immediately. Those two were returned by relatives, saying that the addressees were dead. And even those letters expressed thanks for the little bit of thoughtfulness.

Perhaps the most touching answer came from Bishop William F. McDowell, whose wife had once cared for me with such motherly thoughtfulness that I never forgot it—but I had never written her a letter of thanks. Now I remembered and, knowing that she was gone, wrote my Thanksgiving letter to the bishop, telling him of my memory. I received this in response:

My dear Will:
Your letter was so beautiful, so real, that as I sat reading it in my study tears fell from my eyes, tears of

40

gratitude. Then, before I realized what I was doing, I arose from my chair, called her name and started to show it to her—forgetting that she was gone. You will never know how much your letter has warmed my spirit. I have been walking about in the glow of it all day long.

For years I have continued to write my Thanksgiving month letters and I now have more than 500 of the most beautiful answers anyone has ever received.

A Thanksgiving letter isn't much. Only a few lines are necessary. But the rewards are so great that eternity alone can estimate them. Even now, in moments of discouragement, I go over the responses and drive away darkness by reading a few selected at random. Thanks to the rebuke of a friend, I have learned a little about gratitude.

WILLIAM L. STIDGER

Most smiles are started by another smile.

GOOD READING

My wife had been feeling depressed when I headed off for work one recent morning, but when I returned home in the evening, she was on the top of the world.

"What happened?" I asked, and she pointed to a letter. It was from an old friend of ours, and ended:

> "Don't answer this letter, but pretend you need to, so allot the time. Then use it to gaze into space and acknowledge that you are special — to yourself, and to me."

One sentence, but it changed a day.

J.M.A.

III

Adventures in Friendship

Making Families of Friends

*There are the families we're born into and the ones
formed by friends of the heart. We all need at least
one, and our lives are enriched by many.*

Some days my handwriting resembles my mother's,
slanting hopefully and a bit extravagantly eastward.
Other days it looks more like my father's: resolute,
vertical. Both my parents will remain in my nerves
and muscles and mind until the day I die, and so will
my sister. But they aren't the only ones.

The trouble with the families many of us were born
into is that they are too far away. In emergencies we
rush across continents to their side, as they do to ours.
But our blood kin are often too remote to ease us from
our Tuesdays to our Wednesdays. For this we must
rely on our families of friends.

These new families may consist of either friends of
the road, ascribed by chance, or friends of the heart,
achieved by choice. Friends of the road are those we
happen to go to school with, work with or live near.
They know where we went last weekend and whether
we still have a cold. Just being around gives them a
provisional importance in our lives, and us in theirs. If
we were to move away, six months or two years will
probably erase us from each other's thoughts — unless
we have become friends of the heart.

A friend of the heart is one who perceives me as one
of the better versions of myself. We make good music,

this friend and I, and good silences, too. We phone each other earlier and later than we would dare to bother others. We don't confuse politeness with generosity. At times we argue. We travel together: when cash and time are short, a trip across town will do. Anywhere, just so we can gather, hone and compare our reactions. And, coming and going, we absorb each other's histories.

Friendships are sacred and miraculous, but can be even more so if they lead to the equivalent of clans. As a member in six or seven tribes besides the one I was born into, I have been trying to figure which earmarks are common to both kinds of families. My conclusions:

Good families have a chief, or a heroine or a founder — someone around whom others cluster, whose achievements and example spur them on to like feats. Sometimes clans harbor several such personages at one time.

Good families have a switchboard operator — someone who cannot help but keep track of what all the others are up to, who plays Houston Mission Control to everyone else's Apollo. This role, like the foregoing one, is assumed rather than assigned.

Good families are hospitable. Knowing that hosts need guests as much as guests need hosts, they are generous with honorary memberships for friends. Such clans exude a vivid sense of surrounding rings of relatives, neighbors, teachers, students and godparents, any of whom might break or slide into the inner circle. Inside that circle a wholesome, tacit emotional feudalism develops. This means you can ask me to supervise your children for the two weeks you will be in the hospital, and that however inconvenient this might be for me, I shall manage. It means I can phone you on a dreary, wretched Sunday afternoon, knowing you will tell me to come right over.

Good families deal squarely with direness. Pity the tribe that doesn't have and cherish at least one flamboyant eccentric. Pity, too, the one that supposes it can avoid the woes to which all flesh is heir. Lunacy, bankruptcy, suicide and other unthinkable fates sooner or later afflict the noblest of clans. Family life is a set of givens, and it takes courage to see certain givens as blessings rather than as curses.

Good families prize their rituals. These are vital. They weld a family together, evoke a past, imply a future, hint at continuity. A clan becomes more of a clan each time it gathers to observe a fixed ritual (Christmas, birthdays, Thanksgiving and so on), grieve at a funeral, or when it devises a new rite of its own. But rituals can't be decreed. They emerge at moments that happen only once, around whose memory meanings cluster. You don't choose those moments. They choose themselves.

Good families, not just the blood kind, need to find some way to connect with posterity. What are we who lack children to do? Build houses? Plant trees? Write books or symphonies, or laws? Perhaps. But even so, there still should be children on the sidelines, if not at the center, of our lives. It is a sad impoverishment if we don't regularly see and talk to and laugh with — and make much of — people who can expect to outlive us by several decades.

Good families also honor their elders. The wider the age range, the stronger the tribe. Grandparents now are in much more abundant supply than they were when old age was rarer. If actual grandparents are not at hand, no family should have too hard a time finding substitute ones to whom to give unfeigned homage.

One day in the lobby of a friend's apartment building I watched as two nurses came out of the elevator, one on either side of a wizened, staring woman who couldn't have weighed more than 70 pounds. It was all the woman could do to make her way down three steps to the sidewalk and the curb, where a car waited to take her to a nursing home.

The woman, who was 90, had fallen that morning and hurt herself, the doorman told us. She had lived in the building 40 years. Her relatives all were dead, and her few surviving friends no longer chose to see her.

"But how can that *be*?" I asked my friend. "We could never be that alone, could we?"

"It happens," my friend said.

Maybe we can keep it from happening, by giving more thought to our tribes and our clans and our several kinds of families. No aim seems to be more urgent, nor any achievement more worthy of a psalm.

JANE HOWARD

"I Love You"

The words may not come easily, except to lovers, but there are times when they need to be said to a friend.

At the end of World War II, I received orders to transfer from the merchant vessel I had commanded for many years. I was packed to leave when the chief mate came to my quarters. Some of the crew were outside and wanted to say goodby, he reported. A dozen men were on the lower bridge when I reached it. An old oiler stepped from the group. With the swift gesture of embarrassment he thrust a package into my hand. It contained a watch, inscribed: *To Capt. Geo. Grant Who Has Guided Us Safely Through This War.*

A lump as big as a barge choked me as I surveyed the men. They were a mixture of Latin American nationalities: Costa Rican, Panamanian, Honduran. We had crossed and recrossed the Atlantic together, with bombs for Britain. We had zigzagged around the Pacific, delivering Christmas cheer to our armed forces. We had carried provisions to our Naval vessels during the almost catastrophic kamikaze blockade of Okinawa. We had shared danger, loneliness and fear.

When some would have squandered their money on the "wine, women and song" of ports we visited, I had taken most of it from them and sent it to their families. I had "logged" them when they were unfit for duty, and when they had overstayed their leaves.

When bombs, shells and torpedoes had come danger-
ously close, I had cheered them. Now they floated in a
mist before my eyes.

"Why did you do this?" I blurted.

The old oiler answered, "We love you, sir."

There was another time, later. An aged friend was
dying of leukemia. He had lived an active life as head
of a newspaper syndicate, and a convivial social life.
As a raconteur and singer of ballads, he had few
equals. As a companion, he possessed the qualities of
compassion and understanding that are not given to
many. He knew he was dying. And yet, as we
gathered around the piano at his house one night, he
seemed to symbolize the eternity of life.

Suddenly a strange emotion possessed me. Before it
could be controlled, I took him into my arms and said,
"Gosh! I love you." He stiffened in my embrace as a
man will when another man puts his arms around him.
I thought he would push me away. Then a solitary
tear ran down his cheek, and he relaxed. He punched
me playfully in the stomach, as was his habit. "You
old faker, you," he said.

Next morning he phoned me from the bed that was
to be his deathbed within a month. "I have felt that
way at times," he said quietly. "Never could let go.
Wish I had. Too late now. I love you, you old faker, you."

I love you. Three wonderful words that come easily
to the lips of lovers, but often cling to the tongues of
others when they should go free.

I love you. Three words that hold so much of gratitude, understanding and faith. They should be said.

GEORGE H. GRANT

Have You an Educated Heart?

Last October I sent Crystabel a book. She acknow-
ledged it, and promptly. But two months afterward
she actually wrote me another letter, telling me what
she thought of that book; and she proved, moreover,
that she had read it. Now, I ask you, isn't that a
strange and beautiful experience in this careless world?
Crystabel had the educated heart. To such as possess
the educated heart thanks are something like mort-
gages, to be paid in installments. Why, after five years
Crystabel often refers to a gift that has pleased her. It
is the motive for a gift she cares for, not its value; and
hence her gratefulness.

Everything can be done beautifully by the educated
heart, from the lacing of a shoe so that it won't come
loose to passing the salt before it is asked for. If you
say only "Good morning," it can be done pleasingly.
Observe how the polished actor says it, with that
cheerful rising inflection. Merely to speak distinctly is
a great kindness, I consider. You never have to ask,
"What did you say?" of the educated heart. On the
other hand, very few people ever really listen with
kindly attention. They are usually merely waiting for a
chance to pounce upon you with their own narrative.
Or if they do listen, is your story heard with real
sympathy? Does the face really glow?

Consider the usual birthday gift or Christmas
present. By universal practice it is carefully wrapped in

a pretty paper and tied with ribbon. That package is symbolical of what all friendly acts should be — kindness performed with style. Then what is style in giving? Ah, the educated heart makes it a business to know what his friend really wants. One friend I have to whom I can't express a taste that isn't treasured up against need. I said once that I loved watercress, and lightly wished that I might have it for every meal. Never a meal had I at his table since, without finding watercress bought specially for me.

Do you think it's easy, this business of giving? Verily, giving is as much an art as portrait painting or the making of glass flowers. And imagination can surely be brought to bear. Are you sailing for Brazil? It isn't the basket of fine fruits that brings the tears to your eyes, nor the flowers with trailing yards of red ribbon — all that's ordinary everyday kindness. It's that little purse full of Brazilian currency, bills and small change all ready for you when you go ashore at Rio.

The behavior of the educated heart becomes automatic: you set it in the direction of true kindness and courtesy and after a while it will function without deliberate thought. Such thoughtfulness, such consideration is *not* merely decorative. It is the very essence and evidence of sincerity. Without it all so-called kindness is merely titular and perfunctory.

Suppose I submit your name for membership in a club. Have I done you (or my club) any real service unless I also do my best to see that you are elected? And so if I go to every member of the committee, if I urge all my friends to endorse you, that is merely the completion of my regard for you. It is like salt — "It's what makes potatoes taste bad, if you don't put it on."

No one with the educated heart ever approached a clergyman, or a celebrity, or a long-absent visitor with the shocking greeting: "You don't remember me, do you?" No, he gives his name first. No one with the educated heart ever said, "Now do come and see me, sometime!" The educated heart's way of putting it is apt to be, "How about coming next Wednesday?" And strongly I doubt if the educated heart is ever tardy at an appointment. It knows that if only two minutes late a person has brought just that much less of himself.

Truly nothing is so rare as the educated heart. And if you wonder why, just show a group picture — a banquet or a class photograph. What does every one of us first look at, talk about? Ourself. And that's the reason why most hearts are so unlearned in kindness.

If you want to enlarge that mystic organ whence flows true human kindness, you must cultivate your imagination. You must learn to put yourself in another's place, think his thoughts. The educated heart, remember, does kindness *with style*.

GELETT BURGESS

Shared Joy is double joy and shared sorrow is half-sorrow.

SWEDISH PROVERB

"Lend Me a Cup of Sugar"

When I was a child my father, who was always trying
to improve his job and environment, moved often. By
the time I was grown our family had lived in some 20
towns and cities, next door to all sorts of people. My
mother suffered more than the rest of us from these
frequent changes. Dependent upon neighbors for social
outlet, she was often lonely in a new neighborhood,
grieving the loss of old neighbors and shy about
making overtures to the new ones.

When we moved to Kansas City, Mo., she was
particularly depressed. Kansas City seemed cold and
unfriendly. We lived in a little house on a thickly
populated block. But there we were, six children and
two parents, almost as isolated as the Swiss Family
Robinson.

Then one night there was a timid knock at the back
door. It was a woman from next door, wiping her
hands in her apron. "I'm so sorry to intrude," she said,
"but I'm right in the middle of mixing a cake. Could
you lend me a cup of sugar?"

My mother brightened and gave her the whole
canister.

"I'll bring it back tomorrow, just as soon as Walter
can get to the store," our new neighbor said breath-
lessly.

"No hurry," my mother called cheerily, as our
welcome guest vanished in the darkness.

"Now, wasn't she nice?" my mother said, sitting

down on a kitchen chair to ruminate upon this encounter which seemed to her a major social event.

Indeed it was a great event, for she and the neighbor became lifelong friends, as close and loving as sisters.

Years later our neighbor confided to my mother that she hadn't needed that cup of sugar at all; it was simply her way of making a call, a technique of getting acquainted. Borrowing a cup of sugar has always been a passport into almost any woman's kitchen.

The joy of a new home can never be fulfilled without the comforting proximity of good neighbors. Yet good neighbors never exist unless one helps create them by lending or borrowing a cup of sugar.

Whenever we moved into a new house, my mother would call her six children together and admonish them on pain of a birching to be quiet, and to respect the boundaries of our neighbors' yards.

One of our new neighbors had watched glumly on the day we moved in as the van disgorged the six of us children along with our beaten-up, much-traveled furniture. My mother interpreted his expression as dismay.

For several weeks this man observed our Little Lord Fauntleroy behavior with growing bewilderment. Then one evening he spoke to us over the back fence. "You kids don't make very much noise, do you?"

"No, sir," said my brother. "We're not allowed to."

"I used to have a little boy," he said, "I was making him the biggest squirt gun in the world when he died. What do you say we finish it over here in my shed?"

We worked with him in secrecy when he came home

in the evenings. The base of the gun was a big nickel-plated tube about two feet long, to the end of which he soldered a pinpoint nozzle. When a plunger was fixed in this pipe we had a water cannon that would project a stinging spray from our neighbor's shed right into our own kitchen — as my mother's screams confirmed. "What on earth are you doing?" she shouted, running out on the back porch.

Our neighbor roared with laughter. What a delightful turnabout: Mother had thought her children potential enemies of the neighbors, but lo, we were friends! And despite the drenching, she had to laugh, too. Afterward that neighbor and his wife often spent long summer evenings in the yard with my parents, watching our noisy play. He had lost a child, but he did not pass on the cup of bitterness — he lent us a cup of sugar.

Last summer I dropped in to see an old German neighbor across the street. He proudly showed me his truck garden, flourishing in the midst of drought. He explained that he had watered his half-acre of vegetables mostly by hand, although he is 82 years old. "What a job!" I exclaimed. "It's too much work for a man of your years. You and your wife don't need all those vegetables."

"No," he said. "Ve do it vor the neighbors. Ve grow good friends in the garden, *ja?*" and he laughed while he loaded my arms with cucumbers and tomatoes.

Through the years I have consistently discovered that one never finds good neighbors unless one first *becomes* a good neighbor.

HUBERT KELLEY

When we bought our television set, the neighbors gathered around one Saturday to help us put up the antenna. Since we had only the simplest tools, we weren't making much progress — until a man who was new on the block appeared with an elaborate toolbox, with everything we needed to get the antenna up in record time.

As we stood around congratulating our-selves on this piece of good luck, we asked our new neighbor what he made with such fancy tools. Looking at us all, he smiled and answered slowly, "Friends, mostly."

MRS. GARRELL E. ANTHONY

Enjoy Adventures in Friendliness

Don't miss the fun of talking with strangers. The world is full of people waiting to be spoken to.

The promenade deck of the cruise ship was filled with passengers sunning themselves like happy lizards, in hand-touching twosomes, laughing trios and quartets. Everyone was having a fun-in-the-sun holiday — except me. I sat alone, head lowered over a volume of poetry. I wasn't reading. The book was a prop behind which I hid my shyness.

"There's an empty chair up there with us," a voice said.

I looked up, prepared with my customary "No thank you." But the gray-haired stranger was smiling. I had noticed him the first day out. He apparently was traveling alone, and I had watched in amazement and envy the ease with which he had struck up friendships with nearly everyone on board.

Now he pointed to a group at the other end of the deck. "See that fellow with the cap? He was an officer in the Coast Guard during World War II. He's been telling us what it was like patrolling these waters in a blackout. His wife is a buyer for a children's shop. I think you'll enjoy them."

Before I knew it, I had been drawn into the group. And within a surprisingly short time they had ceased to be forbidding strangers and emerged as individuals. Each had a personal story to tell. And eventually, although it had always been difficult for me to talk with strangers, I found myself — with some prodding from Al — answering questions about my own work.

Throughout that cruise, I never ceased to be astonished by the ease with which Al made friends of strangers. Once, at a gala evening affair, he walked over to a well-known television sportscaster who was standing in chilly isolation. To my surprise, his face soon thawed to a smile, and the two stood engaged in lively talk for 15 to 20 minutes.

"Weren't you afraid he'd snub you?" I asked later.

"Not at all," Al replied. "That man has invested half a lifetime in mastering a subject. Don't you think he's pleased to find someone genuinely interested in his work?

"Approaching a stranger is not really difficult," he went on. "Don't bother with generalities. Try to pick up a clue about his interests. Everyone is an authority on something. The trick is to find what that subject is. Why don't you try your luck?" He paused, then added, "You're a friendly, curious person, yet you act aloof for fear of being snubbed."

Soon I did have occasion to try my luck. I was visiting a village school in New Mexico. As I sat in an anteroom waiting to see one of the teachers, the only other person in the room was a Mexican matron. Our glances crossed, and dropped, with that tentative half-smile with which shy strangers measure one another. I searched for something to say to her. As women, we must have shared some interests and crafts. A word popped into my brain: *sopaipilla*, thin Mexican pancakes which are covered with honey or syrup for a dessert. I told her that I had long looked for the recipe. By the time I was called in for my appointment, I had learned not only her recipe, but that of her mother, grandmother and mother-in-law, and had a tantalizing glimpse into her private — and different — world.

Since then, strangers have been writing my personal encyclopedia. A pearl importer from Texas, on a flight to Montreal, described the difficulties of setting up business in Japan after World War II. I learned about delicate plastic surgery from an Army nurse and the intricacies of the daily double from a horse-playing waiter. One morning I noticed a cabdriver leaning intently toward the radio as a certain song was being played. I asked him about it, and was rewarded with a lively and learned discourse on Israeli folk music.

To discover a stranger's interests, become a book-spy: On a plane or train, notice the titles your seat-mates are reading. You can also learn something about strangers if you have an ear for accents. One rainy afternoon I went into the ladies' room of a large hotel and took off my soaked shoes to dry my feet. As the attendant helped me, I picked up a lilting inflection in her voice, and ventured a guess that she had spent her girlhood in Ireland. The result was an hour's magic as she recalled enchanting tales of her childhood.

The trick of friendliness lies in the attitude with which you face the world around you. A woman famed for the friendliness she inspires once tested her luck by walking into a public place with a downcast face — rather than her usual open, joyful smile. No one greeted her. "I'm thankful," she concluded, "that I am the kind of person who can speak and smile first!"

It still is difficult for me to overcome my reticence. But I intend to keep trying. For I have learned that genuine, friendly interest is the open sesame to one of life's zestful adventures, and that I need not feel alone any more, anywhere on earth.

An elderly woman summed up the traveler's potential friendships, when I asked if she intended to take a trip alone. "No, I don't expect to be alone," she replied. "I haven't seen a train yet that didn't have someone else on it!"

I know now that the world is not filled with strangers. It is full of other people — waiting only to be spoken to.

BETH DAY

After months of the nasty winter weather
that keeps people housebound, my young
bride still hadn't met many of the neighbors.
I came home early one day and saw her going
from door to door, borrowing things. She
returned and busily set about making a cake
with her borrowed ingredients. I was puzzled
— sure that we had such basic stores in our
own pantry. Later that evening, her idea
became clear. She had invited each
contributor to stop over for coffee — and a
warm piece of "Friendship Cake."

DAVID L. WILSON

Recipe for having friends: Be one.

ELBERT HUBBARD

 *This I Believe*

I really believe that every man on this earth is my
brother. He has a soul like mine, the ability to understand friendship, the capacity to create beauty. In all
the continents of this world I have met such men. In
the most savage jungles of New Guinea I have met my
brother and in Tokyo I have seen him clearly walking
before me.

In my brother's house I have lived without fear.

Once in the wildest part of Guadalcanal I had to spend some days with men who still lived and thought in the old stone age, but we got along together fine and I was to see those men in a space of only four weeks ripped from their jungle hideaways and brought down to the airstrips, where some of them learned to drive the ten-ton trucks which carried gasoline to our bombing planes.

Once in India I lived for several days with villagers who didn't know a word of English. But the fact that I couldn't speak their language was no hindrance. Differences in social custom never kept me from getting to know and like savage Melanesians in the New Hebrides. They ate roast dog and I ate Army Spam and if we had wanted to emphasize differences I am sure each of us could have concluded the other was nuts. But we stressed similarities and so long as I could snatch a Navy blanket for them now and then we had a fine old time with no words spoken.

I believe it was only fortunate experience that enabled me to travel among my brothers and to live with them. Therefore I do not believe it is my duty to preach to other people and insist that they also accept all men as their true and immediate brothers. These things come slow. Sometimes it takes lucky breaks to open our eyes. I had to learn gradually, as I believe the world will one day learn.

To my home in rural Pennsylvania come brown men and yellow men and black men from around the world. In *their* countries I lived and ate with them. In *my* country they shall live and eat with me. Until the day I die my home must be free to receive these travelers and it never seems so big a home or so much a place of love as when some man from India or Japan or Mexico or Tahiti or Fiji shares it with me. For on those happy days it reminds me of the wonderful affection I have known throughout the world.

I believe that all men are my brothers. I know it when I see them sharing my home.

JAMES A. MICHENER

How Large a Circle?

He drew a circle that shut me out —
Heretic, rebel, a thing to flout.
But Love and I had the wit to win:
We drew a circle that took him in.

EDWIN MARKHAM

So much of life is spent in keeping other people out of it. Private rooms and houses, private clubs and offices, private roads and beaches — with all of them the point is the same: "This isn't your property. It's mine. Keep out!" Of course, in one sense, a circle that shuts the world out is needed by everyone. We all need places of refuge. We are all porcupines, and our quills are less troublesome if there is a little space around us.

But there is another sense in which the size of a human being can be measured by the circles he draws to take the world in. A few people are too small to draw a circle larger than themselves. Most go a little further and include their families. Still others draw the line at the edges of their own social group or political party, their own race and color, their own religion or nation. The people are too few who have the bigness of interest and compassion to draw a circle large enough for all.

The smaller the circle, the smaller the man. A strong man is not afraid of people different from himself, and a wise man welcomes them. If he knows nothing else, he knows that human beings have no place to live except the earth and that unless we want to die together we must learn to live together. But the wise man probably knows, too, that when he draws a circle to shut out his brother he does less damage to his brother than he does to himself. He puts himself in solitary confinement, and he locks the door from the inside. He denies himself the riches of other men's experience. He starves his own mind, hardens his own heart.

When a wise man names his brothers, he draws no circle smaller than the first one ever drawn on the earth. In the beginning, God gave the world its shape. He made it round.

ROY PEARSON

The Girls' Big Swap

Our youngsters may yet teach us how easy it is to exchange fear for friendship.

Pikes Peak and I stared in amazed disbelief as we watched the Roundup "city" spring into being far below us. The 1200-acre tract at the foot of the mountains north of Colorado Springs burst into a bloom of brilliant-colored tents like prairie flowers after the first rain. Eighty-five hundred Senior Girl Scouts from the United States and its possessions, Girl Guides from all over the world, and 1500 volunteers and staff members had moved in to set up camp. "A Mile High — A World Wide," as the Roundup slogan proclaimed it, the new city was a going concern in one day.

The girls — ages 14 to 18 — were experienced campers who, as a result of their personal achievements, had won the privilege of representing their councils at this super-camping session. As in all Girl Scout activities, the troop was the basic unit of organization. The four patrols in each troop came from widely scattered states; for instance, Scouts from Hawaii, California, New Jersey and Florida might be in one troop.

Observing the Roundup was like trying to watch a 1000-ring circus. The day opened officially with a thrilling spectacle as thousands of youngsters, Western hats atilt, arms swinging, marched over the hills toward the avenue of flags. Standing at attention, they maintained complete silence while their buglers played reveille. Then, as the color guards raised the flags of all the countries in the World Association of Girl Guides and Girl Scouts, and the flags of every state in the Union, an audible sigh of pride swept across the assembly.

Reveille over, the girls marched back to begin a busy day. Swapping was a major activity. Troops back home had spent months preparing swaps for their representatives to trade at Roundup. Reflecting natural resources, history, nature, handicrafts of their communities, swaps provided an instant key to friendship. The variety was endless and ingenious.

"Anybody want to swap for a genuine snake vertebra?" asks a Louisiana girl. A North Carolina girl holds up a long, green, velvety bean. "It's a wisteyreya beeyon," she drawls.

I was curious about the Alaska swaps. "Watch," the girls said. "Here's how we do it." Quickly pulling fur parkas over their heads, they started speaking the Aleut Indian language to a girl who had come up to swap. They winked at me as their visitor politely gestured and spoke slowly, to make these Eskimos understand that she longed for one of their tiny gold pans complete with pick and nugget. She offered in exchange a piece of leather stamped with an authentic Arizona cattle brand. After the trade was made, the girls abandoned their act and started telling their surprised new friend about gold panning in Alaska.

One of the challenges of Roundup was learning to "say it in another language." "The girls from Brazil are giving us a lesson in Portuguese this afternoon," a

Scout from Illinois explained, "and we're going to teach them to splice rope."

At the demonstration area on a hillside overlooking the camp, hundreds of shows took place during Roundup, many simultaneously. Girls from Pueblo, Colo., built an adobe house. North Dakota girls built a sod one — they had brought their own sod. "Our ancestors lived in houses like this. We wanted Scouts from other parts of the country to see one." The air rang with sounds and vibrated with color as patrols did Swedish dances, built a Finnish steam bath, rendered the Lord's Prayer in Indian sign language, made Amish apple butter. Scouts from Hawaii gave lessons in lahala weaving as well as ukulele playing and hula dancing. New England staged a quilting bee; Los Angeles instructed in movie makeup.

Over charcoal broilers, on which they also cooked their meals, the girls demonstrated the preparation of regional delicacies. New Jersey girls, dressed in Dutch costume made holeless doughnuts light as thistledown, called *oliebollen.* A Wisconsin patrol made Lithuanian pastry — and did a dance while it baked. The girls from New Orleans concocted such heavenly gumbo that the commissary had to make special trips to town to keep them supplied with crab and shrimp.

At youth forums the girls swapped ideas with experts in various fields. They asked, "Are parents' attitudes really the problem in human relations?" And, "How can I be proud of my heritage if I deny this same right to others?" It was interesting that they seemed unaware of the race, creed or color of the girls participating in these discussions.

No city ever had a healthier population. There were the usual minor casualties such as sunburn, insect bites and sprains. But Texas was responsible for the only serious epidemic. It broke out the first day, raged through the camps until by noon of the second day every patrol had contracted an incurable case of "Hi, y'all."

On the last night of Roundup the air was soft and a sliver of moon hung over the mountain peaks. A huge campfire blazed high, and the natural arena, filled to the brim with girls, grew hushed as the Girl Guides from abroad filed by. Each carried a scroll which she read, then symbolically placed on the fire in the cause of peace, friendship and tolerance.

I overheard a tiny girl from Korea murmur to her blond companion, "This is the first time I ever left Seoul. After Roundup I will no longer fear foreigners."

"Foreigners!" her companion exclaimed. "There isn't a single foreigner in this whole Roundup, even if parents are from every country in the world."

Our youngsters may yet teach us how easy it is to swap fear for friendship.

MARY BARD

The world is round so that friendship may circle it.

PIERRE TEILHARD DE CHARDIN

 *A Thousand and One Lives*

Each day brings us the chance to forge friendships with people of varied occupations and outlooks. When we accept this challenge, we find that our own lives are enriched beyond measure.

One summer I went on a conducted tour of Switzerland. In Bern, I was detained; no one noticed my absence and the bus left without me. I felt annoyed, but as my party would be returning on the following day I decided to make the best of my enforced stay. I visited the old town clock which produces a procession of antique figures at the striking of the hour, and then walked out to the famous bear pit. Here I asked a bystander where I could get lunch. The Swiss, seeing that I was a stranger, replied: "I am just going home to lunch. Would you like to join me?"

I hesitated at this unlooked-for invitation, but accepted. I was introduced to the man's wife and two young children, and was soon made to feel at home. The Swiss was a watchmaker, and after lunch showed me around his small factory, explaining how the watches were assembled and giving me a chance to meet some of the workmen. When we parted it was on cordial terms and with the promise to keep in touch with each other in the future. Next day I rejoined the escorted tour, far from sorry at an occurrence which had not only gained me a firm friend but had vividly brought home to me an attitude of mind which cramps the lives of many people.

Some of us travel through life on a conducted tour, making friends only with the people inside the bus, keeping to the main roads and well-recognized centers. Then we realize too late that our lives are narrow, and complain that we are not fully living — forgetful of the fact that the remedy lies in our own hands. If we are willing to go off the beaten track, to make friends and acquaintances with people of diverse callings, we shall find our lives immeasurably enriched. In the words of the Arab proverb, "Let a man make varied friends and he will lead a thousand and one lives."

Ever since Aristotle, philosophers have agreed that even more than health or great talents a plenitude of friends is the greatest good in life. Yet, while this lies wholly within our power to secure, how seldom is it used as a working principle in daily life! Few of us really try to extend the circle of our acquaintances in the spirit of Samuel Johnson, who said, "I look upon every day as lost in which I do not make a new acquaintance." Dr. Johnson's friends, as in the case of most people who have had full and rewarding careers, were in all walks of life, for he realized that no one can claim to know life until he knows all types of people.

It is easier than we think to strike up a friendship. Whenever he entered a shop, Daniel Webster used to start a conversation with the storekeeper, asking a question about a fine point involved in the shopkeeper's trade: in grinding coffee, for instance, or selecting a choice cigar. He knew that few people can resist discoursing on a subject in which they are expert; once the ice had been broken in this way he found that other exchanges followed easily and naturally.

Another approach is to express one's appreciation warmly when one receives a service. This breaks down barriers and draws out people more than does an hour of small talk. It was such a compliment that gained me the acquaintance of one of the richest personalities I have ever known — a bootblack in Piccadilly, a tall, weather-beaten old man with a quiet manner. Most of his customers barely exchange a word with him and leave without realizing that they have missed an opportunity of getting to know one of London's most colorful and interesting characters — an ex-member of the Canadian Mounties, a man who speaks five languages and has a fund of fascinating and revealing stories to tell.

In casual encounters no method is more effective than to find common ground with the other person. The mere fact of reading the same newspaper or owning the same make of car can serve as a gangplank to friendship. Another sure way is to remark on some common taste, however trifling. This was Sydney Smith's approach, as his remark to Lady Holland at a dinner party bears witness. "Madam," he said, "all my life I have been looking for a person who dislikes gravy. Let us swear eternal amity."

Despite the rewards of wide friendships many people deny themselves this enrichment of their lives. Some have an idea that they are too good to mix with people outside their own group.

They might ponder the fact that the great figures of history have not considered themselves too good for friendship with any man; on the contrary, they have given freely of themselves to all comers.

There are others who mistakenly believe that only persons with similar interests and objectives can become friends. On the contrary, it is often people from different walks of life who form the closest ties, because each is attracted by the novelty of the other's background and occupation.

Some imagine that friendship is an affair of continual meetings. This is not so; it is a frank exchange of confidence, a sense of comprehension and response which may last a lifetime, transcending space and time. No one led a more remote life than David Livingstone, the explorer, yet he had countless friends. He sent hundreds of letters each year to friends all over the world, many of whom he knew only from a chance and fleeting acquaintance.

To declare that we already have a few old friends, neighbors and business associates and that life does not allow for more is a mistaken view. Nothing is more limiting than a closed circle of acquaintanceship where every avenue of conversation has been explored and social exchanges are fixed in a known routine. Sir William Osler used to say, "A man starts to grow old when he stops making new friends. For this is the sign of development, of assimilating new ideas, of zest for life."

We should never be held back by shyness from encountering strangers. I remember once at a party I proposed to a young student of music that he should meet the distinguished pianist for whom the event had been given. He declined, saying with embarrassment that the celebrity would only be bored by such an introduction.

At dinner after the party the pianist remarked to me: "I saw you talking to a young man this evening. He looked interesting and he had the hands of a musician — I should have liked to meet him." Here was the chance lost of a valuable and influential friendship, and it was one which did not recur.

Each one of us has something unique to offer in the cause of good comradeship. It may be a certain trait of character or an outlook on life or simply a capacity for telling amusing stories, but, whatever it is, we can give freely of that gift each time we make a new acquaintance. By enriching our own lives through wider friendship we also enrich ourselves for our future friends.

Each day presents us with a challenge to turn strange faces into familiar ones. If we take up that challenge, we shall find our own lives grow full beyond measure.

A. J. CRONIN

Friendship is born at that moment when one person says to another, "What! You, too? I thought I was the only one."

C.S. LEWIS

# Anton, Friend of All the World

I should be ungrateful indeed had I forgotten the person who showed me two of the most difficult things on earth: how, by means of an inner freedom, a man can free himself from the strongest power in this world, the power of money; and how a man can live among his fellow human beings without making a single enemy.

I came to know this unique individual in a very simple way. One afternoon I was taking my spaniel for a walk, when the dog began to behave strangely. He rolled frenziedly on the ground, rubbed himself against every tree, whimpered and growled incessantly.

While I was wondering what was the matter with him, I became aware that someone was walking by my side — a man of about 30, poorly dressed. A beggar, I thought, and was about to put my hand in my pocket. But the stranger smiled tranquilly at me out of clear blue eyes as though we were old friends. "He's got a tick, poor chap," he said, pointing to my dog. "Come along, we'll have it out."

He addressed me with the *"Du"* which in German is employed only among people who are on intimate terms; but there was such warm friendliness in his gaze that I took no offense at his familiarity. I followed him to a park bench and sat down beside him. He called the dog with a shrill whistle.

And, my Kaspar, who was usually wary of
strangers, responded at once, and, at a sign, put his
head on the man's knee. Searching the dog's coat with
long, sensitive fingers, the stranger finally uttered a
satisfied "Aha!" and began what must have been a
painful operation, for Kaspar whimpered several
times. Yet he made no effort to wriggle free. Suddenly
the man released him. "Here it is," he laughed,
triumphantly holding something in the air. "Now run
along, doggie." As the dog scurried off, the stranger
rose with a nod and walked on. His departure was so
sudden that it did not occur to me until later that I
should have given him something for his trouble, or at
least should have thanked him. But there was the same
finality and self-possession about his going as his coming.

At home I reported the adventure to our cook. "Oh,
that was Anton," she remarked. "He's got an eye for
everything." I asked what he did for a living.
"Nothing," she said, as if astonished by my question.
"What does he want with a job?"

"Well," I said, "everyone has to have something to
live on."

"Not Anton," she said. "Everyone is glad to give
him whatever he wants. He doesn't care about money;
he doesn't need it."

Well, this was odd. I knew that in our little town, as
in every other town in the world, every crust of bread,
every night's lodging and every coat had to be paid
for. How could this spare little fellow with the thread-
bare trousers get around this law, and yet remain
utterly carefree and happy?

I resolved to investigate his technique, and soon dis-

covered that Anton had no kind of settled job. He just
wandered about the town all day long — apparently
aimlessly, but with watchful eyes that observed everything. He would notice the rotting wood in a fence and
call on the owner to suggest that it ought to be
painted. Usually he'd be asked to do the job — for
everybody knew that there was no cupidity in his
suggestions, but only sincere friendliness.

Once I found him sitting in a shoemaker's shop
mending shoes, once acting as an extra waiter at a
party, once taking some children out for a walk. I
discovered that everyone turned to Anton in an
emergency; on one occasion I saw him selling apples
among the market women, and I learned that the
owner of the stall was in childbed and had let him take
her place.

Of course, there are plenty of handy men in every
town, ready to pick up any odd job. The unique thing
about Anton was that, regardless of how hard he had
worked, he firmly refused to accept more money than
he needed for that day. When things went well, he
accepted no payment whatever. "I'll come to you later
if I need anything," he would say.

I soon became aware that this odd, ragged, friendly
fellow had discovered for himself a new system. He
had faith in the decency of human beings; instead of
depositing money in a savings bank, he preferred to
accumulate moral obligations with his fellow towns-
people; he invested his little all in invisible credits
— and even the most cynical could not escape feeling
indebted to one who did things for them as a favor,
without thought of fixed compensation.

One had only to watch Anton walking down the street to realize in what special esteem people held him. Everyone greeted him cordially; everyone shook him by the hand. And this simple, carefree man in the shabby coat walked through the town like a landowner inspecting his estates, with a genial and friendly air. He could enter any door, sit down at any table; everything was his to command. Never have I understood so well the power wielded by one who has mastered the secret of taking no thought for the morrow, and of genuinely trusting in God.

I must frankly admit that it annoyed me at first, after the episode with Kaspar, to have Anton pass me with merely a casual greeting, as though I were more or less a stranger. Evidently he did not wish to presume on that little service. And so the next time something was out of order in the house — water was dripping from a gutter — I suggested to my cook that she send for Anton.

"You can't send for him; he never stays long enough in one place," she replied. "But I'll get word to him." Thus I learned that this strange individual had no home. Yet no one was easier to get in touch with; a sort of wireless telephone connected him with the whole town. It was sufficient to tell the first person you met in the street, "I want Anton," and the word would pass along, until someone ran across him. Indeed, that very afternoon he turned up. He looked at everything with shrewd eyes, pointing out, as he walked through the garden, that here a bush wanted trimming, there a young tree needed transplanting. Finally he inspected the gutter and set to work forthwith.

Two hours later he reported that the job was finished, and departed — again before I could thank him. But this time at least I had told the cook to pay him well. I asked her if he had been satisfied. "Of course, he's always satisfied," she said. "I wanted to give him six shillings, but he would take only two. That would see him through for today and tomorrow. But if the Herr Doktor, he said, ever had an old winter coat to spare —"

I find it hard to describe the pleasure it gave me to be able to offer to this man — the first person I had ever known who took less than was given him, something he was eager to have. I ran after him, "Anton, Anton," I called down the hill. "I have a coat for you." Once more I encountered that serene, tranquil light in his eyes. He was not in the least surprised that I should run after him. It was natural to him that someone who had a coat that was not needed should offer it to another who badly wanted one.

I got the cook to fetch all my available old clothes. He scrutinized the pile, picked up a coat, tried it on and then said quietly, "Yes, this will do me." He said it with the air of a gentleman who has decided to take one of the articles brought out for his inspection in a shop. Then he glanced at the other things. "You can give those shoes to Fritz in the Salsergrasse, he needs a pair; and the shirts to Josef in the Square, he can patch them for himself. If you like I'll take them along for you." This in the magnanimous tone of one volunteering to do a favor; I felt I ought to thank him for distributing my belongings among people who were complete strangers to me. As he tied the things in a bundle, he added, "Yes, you're a good fellow. Nice of you to give all these things away." And he vanished.

Strange, no enthusiastic review of any of my books had ever delighted me so much as this naive praise. In later years I have often thought of this Anton, and always with gratitude, for few people have given me so much spiritual help. Frequently when I have been worrying about stupid little money matters I have called to mind this man who lived calmly and confidently for the day, because he wanted no more than was enough for that one day. And always I have thought: "If everyone were to learn this secret of mutual trust and confidence, there would be no police, no courts of law, no prisons and no money. Would not our whole complicated economic system be remedied if everyone lived like this one man, who gave as much of himself as he could, yet took only what he needed?"

For some years I have heard nothing of Anton. But there are few people about whom I feel less anxiety: I know that God will never leave this man in the lurch and — what's more — men will not, either.

STEFAN ZWEIG

IV

A Friend in Need

Drama at Gate 67

In the jammed airport lounge, the homebound soldier, told there was no room for him on the flight he had to make, looked around the room frantically, as if searching for one friendly face.

The surge of holiday traffic would have taxed the congested Atlanta airport under the best of circumstances. But, as Christmas neared, nature had added an ice storm that stranded thousands of travelers.

As the midnight hour tolled, weary pilgrims clustered around ticket counters, conferring anxiously with agents whose cheeriness had long since evaporated; they, too, longed to be home. Others gathered at the newsstands to thumb silently through paperback books. A few managed to doze, contorted into human pretzels, in uncomfortable seats.

If there was a common bond among this diverse throng, it was loneliness — pervasive, inescapable, suffocating loneliness. But airport decorum required that each traveler maintain his invisible barrier against all the others. Better to be lonely than to be involved, which inevitably meant listening to complaints, and heaven knows everyone had enough complaints of his own already.

Just beneath the surface, in fact, lurked a competitive hostility. After all, there were more passengers than seats; when an occasional plane managed to break out, more travelers stayed behind than made it aboard. "Standby," "Reservation Confirmed," "First Class Passenger" were words that settled priorities and bespoke money, power, influence, foresight — or the lack thereof.

Gate 67 was a microcosm of the whole cavernous airport. Scarcely more than a glassed-in cubicle, it was jammed with travelers hoping to fly to New Orleans, Dallas and points west.

Except for the fortunate few traveling in pairs, there was little conversation. A salesman stared absently into space, as if resigned. A young mother cradled an infant to her breast, gently rocking in a vain effort to soothe the soft whimpering.

And there was a man in a finely tailored suit who somehow seemed impervious to the collective suffering. There was a certain indifference about his manner. He was absorbed in some arcane paper work. Figuring the year-end corporate profits, perhaps. A nerve-frayed traveler sitting nearby, observing this busy man, might have indulged in a cynical fantasy: "His clothes are different, but he can't disguise his nature. It's Ebenezer Scrooge."

Suddenly, the sullen silence was broken by a commotion. A young man in uniform, no more than 19 years old, was in animated conversation with the desk agent. The boy held a low-priority ticket. But he must, he pleaded, get to New Orleans, so that he could take the bus on to the obscure Louisiana village he called home.

The agent wearily told him the prospects were poor for the next 24 hours, maybe longer.

The boy grew frantic. He was soon to be sent to Vietnam. If he did not make this flight, he might never again spend Christmas at home.

Even the businessman looked up from his cryptic computations to show a guarded interest. The agent clearly was moved, even a bit embarrassed. But he could offer only sympathy, not hope. The boy hovered about the departure desk, casting wild and anxious looks around the crowded room, as if seeking but one friendly face.

Finally, the agent hoarsely announced that the flight was ready for boarding. The pilgrims heaved themselves up, gathered their belongings, and shuffled down the small corridor to the waiting craft. Twenty, 30, 100 — until there were no more seats. The agent turned to the frantic young man and shrugged.

Inexplicably, the businessman had lingered behind. Now he stepped forward. "I have a confirmed ticket," he quietly told the agent. "I'd like to give my seat to this young man."

The agent stared incredulously; then he motioned to the soldier. Unable to speak, tears streaming down his face, the boy in olive drab shook hands with the man in gray flannel, who simply murmured, "Good luck. Have a fine Christmas. Good luck."

As the plane door closed and the engines began their rising whine, the businessman turned away, clutching his briefcase, and trudged toward the all-night coffee bar.

No more than a few among the thousands stranded there at the Atlanta airport witnessed the drama at Gate 67. But for these, the sullenness, the frustration, the hostility, all dissolved into a glow.

The lights of the departing plane blinked, starlike, as the craft moved off into the darkness. The infant slept silently now on the breast of the young mother. Perhaps another flight would be leaving before many more hours; but those who saw were less impatient. The glow lingered, gently and pervasively, in that small glass-and-plastic stable at Gate 67.

RAY JENKINS

Friend in Need

When I was young, I believed that I was strong and self-sufficient. I was prepared for disappointment, possibly tragedy. When they came, I'd handle them personally, with style. Nothing could daunt *me*.

Now I am older. I have met with poverty, flood, famine, hurricane, brutalizing labor and illness.

Though the joys have far outweighed the sorrows, there have been times when I was fair-to-middlin' desperate.

There was the time when my husband, my year-old baby and I had one meal a day. We ate baked potatoes and salt. But my neighbor, Alice Miller, provided me with six oranges and six quarts of milk a week for the baby.

Then there was the December evening when my world seemed ended. My husband and I were relaxing before the open fire. We'd spent the day snugging down the cabin for winter, and we felt good, knowing that there were 40 miles of lake and impossible road between us and the nearest settlement. We were laughing over a silly joke. "Louise, you gorgeous fool!" he said—and those were his last words. He died that night. I don't know how I could have survived if it hadn't been for Alys Parsons. She came and sat with me, not saying a word, just being *there*.

After that came the time when I owed a lot of money. I went to each of the people and explained that I couldn't pay now, but if they'd give me a breathing space, I'd pay it later with interest. They all gave me the same answer: "Mrs. Rich, take your time—and forget the interest."

So now I have grown up. I don't believe in myself any more; not in myself alone. I do believe in the decency and sympathy and kindness of every man and woman and child that I meet. I believe also that I have an obligation. Whenever I see anyone in trouble, I am privileged to have the opportunity to repay in a small measure my debt to the people who have helped me. I believe in humanity.

LOUISE DICKINSON RICH

One does not make friends;
one recognizes them.
ISABEL PATERSON

The Soft Answer

*A wise old gentleman teaches us an unforgettable
lesson in friendship.*

The train clanked and rattled through the suburbs of
Tokyo on a drowsy spring afternoon. Our car was
comparatively empty — a few housewives with their
kids in tow, some old folks going shopping.

At one station the doors opened, and suddenly the
quiet was shattered by a man bellowing violent,
incomprehensible curses. The man staggered into our
car. He wore laborer's clothing, and he was big, drunk
and dirty. Screaming, he swung at a woman holding a
baby. The blow sent her spinning into the laps of an
elderly couple. It was a miracle that the baby was
unharmed.

Terrified, the couple jumped up and scrambled
toward the other end of the car. The laborer aimed a
kick at the retreating back of the old woman but
missed as she scuttled to safety. This so enraged the
drunk that he grabbed the metal pole in the center of
the car and tried to wrench it out of its stanchion. The
train lurched ahead, the passengers frozen with fear. I
stood up.

I was young then and in pretty good shape. I'd been
putting in eight hours of aikido training nearly every
day for the past three years. I liked to throw and
grapple. I thought I was tough. Trouble was, my

martial skill was untested in actual combat. As students of aikido, we were not allowed to fight.

"Aikido," my teacher had said again and again, "is the art of reconciliation. Whoever has the mind to fight has broken his connection with the universe. If you try to dominate people, you are already defeated. We study how to resolve conflict, not how to start it."

I listened to his words. I tried hard. I even went so far as to cross the street to avoid the punks who lounged around the train stations. My forbearance exalted me. In my heart, however, I wanted an absolutely legitimate opportunity whereby I might save the innocent by destroying the guilty.

This is it! I said to myself as I got to my feet. *People are in danger. If I don't do something fast, somebody will probably get hurt.*

Seeing me stand up, the drunk recognized a chance to focus his rage. "Aha!" he roared. "A foreigner! You need a lesson in Japanese manners!"

I held on lightly to the commuter strap overhead and gave him a slow look of disgust and dismissal. I planned to take this turkey apart, but he had to make the first move. I wanted him mad, so I pursed my lips and blew him an insolent kiss.

"All right!" he hollered. "You're gonna get a lesson." He gathered himself for a rush at me.

A split second before he could move, someone shouted "Hey!" It was earsplitting. I remember the strangely joyous, lilting quality of it — as though you and a friend had been searching diligently for something, and he had suddenly stumbled upon it. "Hey!"

I wheeled to my left, the drunk spun to his right. We

both stared down at a little old Japanese. He must have been well into his seventies, this tiny gentleman, sitting there immaculate in his kimono. He took no notice of me, but beamed delightedly at the laborer, as though he had a most important, most welcome secret to share.

"C'mere," the old man said in an easy vernacular, beckoning to the drunk. "C'mere and talk with me." He waved his hand lightly.

The big man followed, as if on a string. He planted his feet belligerently in front of the old gentleman, and roared, "Why should I talk to you?" The drunk now had his back to me. If his elbow moved so much as a millimeter, I'd drop him in his socks.

The old man continued to beam at the laborer. "What'cha been drinkin'?" he asked, his eyes sparkling with interest. "I been drinkin' sake," the laborer bellowed back.

"Oh, that's wonderful," the old man said, "absolutely wonderful! You see, I love sake too. Every night, me and my wife (she's 76, you know), we warm up a little bottle of sake and take it out into the garden, and we sit on an old wooden bench. We watch the sun go down, and we look to see how our persimmon tree is doing. My great-grandfather planted that tree, and we worry about whether it will recover from those ice storms we had last winter. Our tree has done better than I expected, though, especially when you consider the poor quality of the soil. It is gratifying to watch when we take our sake and go out to enjoy the evening — even when it rains!" He looked up at the laborer, eyes twinkling.

As he struggled to follow the old man's conversation, the drunk's face began to soften. His fists slowly unclenched. "Yeah," he said. "I love persimmons too...." His voice trailed off.

"Yes," said the old man, smiling, "and I'm sure you have a wonderful wife."

"No," replied the laborer. "My wife died." Very gently, the big man began to sob. "I don't got no *wife*, I don't got no *home*, I don't got no *job*. I'm so *ashamed* of myself." Tears rolled down his cheeks; a spasm of despair rippled through his body.

Now it was my turn. Standing there in my well-scrubbed youthful innocence, my make-this-world-safe-for-democracy righteousness, I suddenly felt dirtier than he was.

Then the train arrived at my stop. As the doors opened, I heard the old man cluck sympathetically. "My, my," he said, "that is a difficult predicament, indeed. Sit down here and tell me about it."

I turned my head for one last look. The laborer was sprawled on the seat, his head in the old man's lap. The old man was softly stroking the filthy, matted hair.

As the train pulled away, I sat down on a bench. What I had wanted to do with muscle had been accomplished with kind words. I had just seen aikido tried in combat, and the essence of it was love.

TERRY DOBSON

This Man Is My Friend

One example of friendship remains with me
as vividly as the moment I first heard of it as
a boy. In his first seasons with the Brooklyn
Dodgers, Jackie Robinson, the first black man
to play Major League baseball, faced venom
nearly everywhere he traveled—fastballs at
his head, spikings on the bases, brutal
epithets from the opposing dugouts and from
the crowds. During one game in Boston, the
taunts and racial slurs seemed to reach a
peak. In the midst of this, another Dodger, a
Southern white named Pee Wee Reese, called
timeout. He walked from his position at
shortstop toward Robinson at second base,
put his arm around Robinson's shoulder, and
stood there with him for what seemed like a
long time. The gesture spoke more eloquently
than the words: this man is my friend.

WILLIE MORRIS

A Kindness Returned

"How can I ever thank you?" my new friend said softly. . . . After nearly 21 years, she found a way.

At the time my son was born, I shared a hospital room with a young woman who bore a son on the same day. Partly because my parents owned a florist shop, the room was soon filled with the lovely scent of roses.

As the seventh floral arrangement was brought in, I was beginning to feel uncomfortable, for no flowers had arrived for my roommate, Ann. She sat on the edge of her bed and leaned forward to admire the latest bouquet. She was a pretty young woman, yet there was something about her large, brown eyes that made me think she had known too much struggling, too much sadness for one so young. I had the feeling she had always had to admire someone else's flowers.

"I'm enjoying every minute of this," she said as though she had read my thoughts and was trying to reassure me. "Wasn't I the lucky one to get you for a roommate?"

I still felt uncomfortable, however. If only there were some magic button I could push to take away the sadness in her eyes. *Well,* I thought, *at least I can see that she has some flowers.* When my mother and father came to see me that day, I asked them to send her some.

The flowers arrived just as Ann and I were finishing supper.

"Another bouquet for you," she said, laughing.

"No, not this time," I said, looking at the card. "These are for you."

Ann stared at the blossoms a long time, not saying anything. She ran her fingers across the pale-blue ceramic bootee and lightly touched each of the sweetheart roses nestled inside as though trying to engrave them on her memory.

"How can I ever thank you?" she said softly when she finally spoke.

I was almost embarrassed. It was such a little kindness on my part.

The son born to my husband and me that day turned out to be our only child. For nearly 21 years he filled our lives with love and laughter, making us feel complete. But on an Easter morning, after a long, painful battle with cancer, he died quietly in our arms.

At the funeral home I was alone with my son in a room filled with the scent of roses, when a deliveryman brought in a tiny bouquet. I didn't read the card until later, as we rode to the cemetery. "To W. John Graves," the card said, "from the boy who was born with you at Memorial Hospital, and his mother."

Only then did I recognize the ceramic bootee I had given to a sad young woman so many years ago, now once again filled with roses. Ann and I had long since lost touch. She had never known our son, never been aware of his illness. She must have read his obituary in a newspaper. I passed the card on to my mother sitting beside me. She, too, remembered.

"A kindness returned," Mother said.

A few days later, my husband and I, with several members of our family, went to the cemetery to clear John's grave. The bootee of roses sat at its foot, towered over by tall wreaths and sprays.

"How odd that anyone would send something like that to a funeral," someone said. "It seems more appropriate for a birth."

"There *was* a birth," said my husband quietly. "John was born into Eternal Life." I looked at him with surprise, knowing those words were difficult for a man who had never spoken openly about such matters.

He emptied out the flowers and handed me the ceramic bootee. I held it and, just as Ann had done, I traced it with my fingers, thinking of all the messages it contained: the embers of friendship that glow through the years, gratitude remembered and, beneath it all, the promise of Resurrection, which comforts us now.

VIRGINIA HALL GRAVES

Strangers are friends that you have yet to meet.

ROBERTA LIEBERMAN

Acknowledgments

Grateful acknowledgment is made to the following organizations and individuals for permission to reprint.

"Yonder's My Best Friend" by Rob Wood. © 1968 by The Reader's Digest Association, Inc.

"The Stranger Who Taught Magic" by Arthur Gordon. © 1970 by The Reader's Digest Association, Inc.

"On the Dunes" reprinted with permission of Macmillan Publishing Co., Inc. from *Collected Poems of Sara Teasdale*. Copyright © 1920 by Macmillan Publishing Co., Inc., renewed 1948 by Mamie T. Wheless.

Willie Morris in Parade. Copyright © 1980 by Willie Morris.

"Information Please" by Paul Villiard. © 1966 by The Reader's Digest Association, Inc.

D.R.R. © 1966 by The Reader's Digest Association, Inc.

"Friendship" by John W. Walker. © 1982 by The Reader's Digest Association, Inc.

"Mail Call!" by Joan Mills. © 1981 by The Reader's Digest Association, Inc.

"A Letter to Walter" by Charlton Ogburn Jr. © 1966 by The Reader's Digest Association, Inc.

Clifton Simer in The Rotarian. Copyright © 1954 by The Rotarian, Evanston, Ill. 60201

"The Thanksgiving Letters" by William Stidger. Christian Advocate, Nashville, Tenn. 37202

Good Reading. Copyright © 1977 by Good Reading, Litchfield, Ill. 62056

"You Are Special" by J.M.A. © 1978 by The Reader's Digest Association, Inc.

Making Families of Friends by Jane Howard. Copyright © 1978 by Jane Howard. Reprinted by permission of Simon & Schuster.

"I Love You" by George H. Grant. © 1962 by The Reader's Digest Association, Inc.

Have You an Educated Heart? by Gelett Burgess. Copyright © 1923 by Viking Penguin Inc.

"Lend Me a Cup of Sugar" by Hubert Kelley. © 1959 by The Reader's Digest Association, Inc.

Book design by Betsy Beach
Cover design by Patrice Barrett
Cover photograph by Beth Welsh
Book type set in Palatino; Cover type set in Romic

200
Bow

Date Due

Code 4386-04, CLS-4, Broadman Supplies, Nashville, Tenn.,
Printed in U.S.A.